Catholic
Prayer Journal

CATHOLIC PRAYER JOURNAL

Weekly journal for Catholics
Second Edition 2022

Cover and interior design
Marlene Amparan

"

He who carries
God in his heart
bears Heaven with him
wherever he goes.

St. Ignatius of Loyola

This journal belongs to:

_____

My Catholic
PRAYER JOURNAL

SCRIPTURE

WHAT VERSE OUT OF TODAY'S SCRIPTURE
READING WOULD YOU LIKE TO
DIG INTO FURTHER?

- Make some observations about your chosen portion of Scripture.
- Then write what you observe in the text and its meaning.

APPLICATION

CONSIDER HOW THE TEACHING
CONNECTS TO YOUR LIFE

- Apply God's Word to your life.
- What changes would you like to make in your life based on this passage?

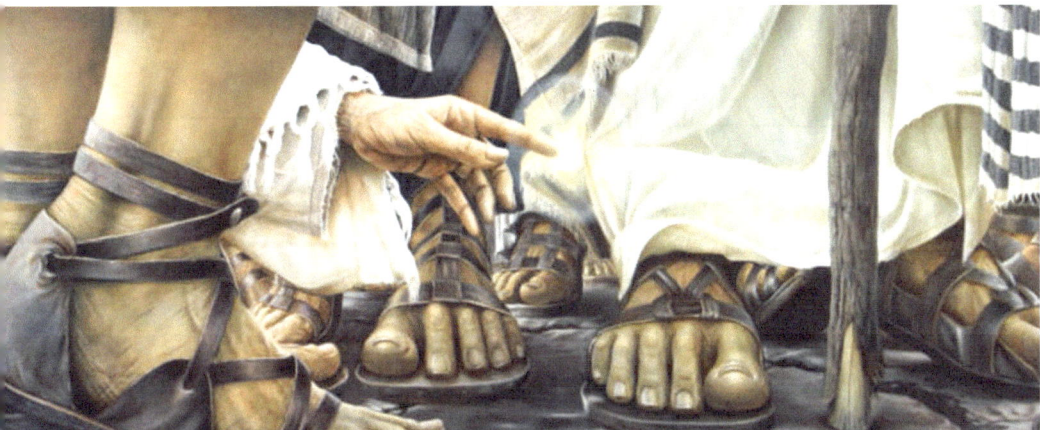

PRAYER

WRITE DOWN A PRAYER TO GOD IN RESPONSE TO HIS WORD

- Once written down, pray those words to God either out loud or silently.

PRAY THE EXAMEN

ST. IGNATIUS OF LOYOLA'S EXAMEN IS AN OPPORTUNITY FOR PEACEFUL DAILY REFLECTIVE PRAYER.

- Find the movement of God in all the people and events of your day.
- The Examen is a set of introspective prompts for you to follow or adapt to your own character and spirit.

Art: "Encounter" by Daniel Cariola

Pray the Examen
of St. Ignatius of Loyola

GRATITUDE

1 Place yourself in God's presence.
Give thanks for God's great love for you.

GRACE

2 Pray for the grace to understand how God is acting in your life.

REVIEW

3 Review your day — recall specific moments and your feelings at the time.

REPENT

4 Reflect on what you did, said, or thought in those instances.
Were you drawing closer to God, or further away?

RESOLVE

5 Look toward tomorrow — think of how you might collaborate more effectively with God's plan.
Be specific, and conclude with the "Our Father."

Take Lord, and receive all my liberty, my memory, my understanding, and my entire will, all that I have and possess. Thou hast given all to me. To Thee, O lord, I return it. All is Thine, dispose of it wholly according to Thy will. Give me Thy love and thy grace, for this is sufficient for me.

St. Ignatius of Loyola

"AM I NOT HERE WHO AM YOUR MOTHER?"

Our Lady of Guadalupe

> " God would never inspire
> me with desires which
> cannot be realized; so
> in spite of my littleness,
> I can hope to be a saint.
> St. Therese of Lisieux

My prayer
journal

30 day challenge

Opening Prayer

Scripture & Reflection

Write down the Bible passage and your reflection.

Observation

Application

Apply God's Word to your life.

Today I will...

Prayer

Write down a prayer to God in response to His Word.

Pray the Examen

Reflect prayerfully on God's presence during your day.

Gratitude

Grace

Review

Repent

Resolve

My prayer
journal

30 day challenge

Opening Prayer

Scripture & Reflection
Write down the Bible passage and your reflection.

Observation

Application
Apply God's Word to your life.

Today I will...

Prayer

Write down a prayer to God in response to His Word.

Pray the Examen

Reflect prayerfully on God's presence during your day.

Gratitude

Grace

Review

Repent

Resolve

My prayer
journal

30 day challenge

Opening Prayer

Scripture & Reflection

Write down the Bible passage and your reflection.

Observation

Application

Apply God's Word to your life.

Today I will...

Prayer

Write down a prayer to God in response to His Word.

Pray the Examen

Reflect prayerfully on God's presence during your day.

Gratitude

Grace

Review

Repent

Resolve

My prayer
journal

30 day challenge

🕊 Opening Prayer

Scripture & Reflection
Write down the Bible passage and your reflection.

Observation

Application
Apply God's Word to your life.

Today I will...

Prayer

Write down a prayer to God in response to His Word.

Pray the Examen

Reflect prayerfully on God's presence during your day.

Gratitude

Grace

Review

Repent

Resolve

My prayer journal

30 day challenge

Opening Prayer

Scripture & Reflection

Write down the Bible passage and your reflection.

Observation

Application

Apply God's Word to your life.

Today I will...

Prayer

Write down a prayer to God in response to His Word.

Pray the Examen

Reflect prayerfully on God's presence during your day.

Gratitude

Grace

Review

Repent

Resolve

My prayer journal

30 day challenge

▯▯▯▯▯▯▯▯▯▯▯▯▯▯▯▯▯▯▯▯▯▯▯▯▯▯▯▯▯▯

Opening Prayer

Scripture & Reflection

Write down the Bible passage and your reflection.

Observation

Application

Apply God's Word to your life.

Today I will...

Prayer

Write down a prayer to God in response to His Word.

Pray the Examen

Reflect prayerfully on God's presence during your day.

Gratitude

Grace

Review

Repent

Resolve

My prayer *journal*

30 day challenge

Opening Prayer

Scripture & Reflection

Write down the Bible passage and your reflection.

Observation

Application

Apply God's Word to your life.

Today I will...

Prayer

Write down a prayer to God in response to His Word.

Pray the Examen

Reflect prayerfully on God's presence during your day.

Gratitude

Grace

Review

Repent

Resolve

I'm grateful for

Prayer intentions

> "
> Whatever you ask for
> in prayer with faith,
> you will receive.
>
> *Matthew 21:22*

BE NOT AFRAID ... OPEN WIDE THE DOORS TO CHRIST!

St. John Paul II

My prayer
journal

Date **S M T W T F S**

30 day challenge

Opening Prayer

Scripture & Reflection
Write down the Bible passage and your reflection.

Observation

Application
Apply God's Word to your life.

Today I will...

Prayer

Write down a prayer to God in response to His Word.

Pray the Examen

Reflect prayerfully on God's presence during your day.

Gratitude

Grace

Review

Repent

Resolve

My prayer journal

Date S M T W T F S

30 day challenge

Scripture & Reflection

Write down the Bible passage and your reflection.

Opening Prayer

Observation

Application

Apply God's Word to your life.

Today I will...

Prayer

Write down a prayer to God in response to His Word.

Pray the Examen

Reflect prayerfully on God's presence during your day.

Gratitude

Grace

Review

Repent

Resolve

My prayer
journal

30 day challenge

Opening Prayer

Scripture & Reflection
Write down the Bible passage and your reflection.

Observation

Application
Apply God's Word to your life.

Today I will...

Prayer

Write down a prayer to God in response to His Word.

Pray the Examen

Reflect prayerfully on God's presence during your day.

Gratitude

Grace

Review

Repent

Resolve

My prayer *journal*

30 day challenge

Opening Prayer

Scripture & Reflection

Write down the Bible passage and your reflection.

Observation

Application

Apply God's Word to your life.

Today I will...

Prayer

Write down a prayer to God in response to His Word.

Pray the Examen

Reflect prayerfully on God's presence during your day.

Gratitude

Grace

Review

Repent

Resolve

My prayer journal

30 day challenge

Opening Prayer

Scripture & Reflection
Write down the Bible passage and your reflection.

Observation

Application
Apply God's Word to your life.

Today I will...

Prayer

Write down a prayer to God in response to His Word.

Pray the Examen

Reflect prayerfully on God's presence during your day.

Gratitude

Grace

Review

Repent

Resolve

My prayer
journal

30 day challenge

Opening Prayer

Scripture & Reflection
Write down the Bible passage and your reflection.

Observation

Application
Apply God's Word to your life.

Today I will...

Prayer

Write down a prayer to God in response to His Word.

Pray the Examen

Reflect prayerfully on God's presence during your day.

Gratitude

Grace

Review

Repent

Resolve

My prayer
journal

30 day challenge

Opening Prayer

Scripture & Reflection
Write down the Bible passage and your reflection.

Observation

Application
Apply God's Word to your life.

Today I will...

Prayer

Write down a prayer to God in response to His Word.

Pray the Examen

Reflect prayerfully on God's presence during your day.

Gratitude

Grace

Review

Repent

Resolve

OUR FATHER

I'm thankful for: *I ask you for:*

1

2

3

4

5

6

7

8

9

10

Especially: *Especially:*

"He who wishes for anything but Christ, does not know what he
wishes; he who asks for anything but Christ, does not know what
he is asking; he who works, and not for Christ,
does not know what he is doing."

St. Philip Neri

Pray, hope and don't worry. Worry is useless. Our Merciful Lord will listen to your prayer.

St. Pio of Pietrelcina

My prayer
journal

30 day challenge

Opening Prayer

Scripture & Reflection
Write down the Bible passage and your reflection.

Observation

Application
Apply God's Word to your life.

Today I will...

Prayer

Write down a prayer to God in response to His Word.

Pray the Examen

Reflect prayerfully on God's presence during your day.

Gratitude

Grace

Review

Repent

Resolve

My prayer
journal

30 day challenge

🕊 Opening Prayer

Scripture & Reflection
Write down the Bible passage and your reflection.

Observation

Application
Apply God's Word to your life.

Today I will...

Prayer

Write down a prayer to God in response to His Word.

Pray the Examen

Reflect prayerfully on God's presence during your day.

Gratitude

Grace

Review

Repent

Resolve

My prayer
journal

Date   S M T W T F S

30 day challenge
□□□□□□□□□□□□□□□□□□□□□□□□□□□□□□

Opening Prayer

Scripture & Reflection
Write down the Bible passage and your reflection.

Observation

Application
Apply God's Word to your life.

Today I will...

Prayer

Write down a prayer to God in response to His Word.

Pray the Examen

Reflect prayerfully on God's presence during your day.

Gratitude

Grace

Review

Repent

Resolve

My prayer
journal

30 day challenge

Opening Prayer

Scripture & Reflection
Write down the Bible passage and your reflection.

Observation

Application
Apply God's Word to your life.

Today I will...

Prayer

Write down a prayer to God in response to His Word.

Pray the Examen

Reflect prayerfully on God's presence during your day.

Gratitude

Grace

Review

Repent

Resolve

My prayer *journal*

30 day challenge

Opening Prayer

Scripture & Reflection

Write down the Bible passage and your reflection.

Observation

Application

Apply God's Word to your life.

Today I will...

Prayer

Write down a prayer to God in response to His Word.

Pray the Examen

Reflect prayerfully on God's presence during your day.

Gratitude

Grace

Review

Repent

Resolve

My prayer
journal

30 day challenge

Opening Prayer

Scripture & Reflection
Write down the Bible passage and your reflection.

Observation

Application
Apply God's Word to your life.

Today I will...

Prayer

Write down a prayer to God in response to His Word.

Pray the Examen

Reflect prayerfully on God's presence during your day.

Gratitude

Grace

Review

Repent

Resolve

My prayer
journal

30 day challenge

🕊️ Opening Prayer

Scripture & Reflection
Write down the Bible passage and your reflection.

Observation

Application
Apply God's Word to your life.

Today I will...

Prayer

Write down a prayer to God in response to His Word.

Pray the Examen

Reflect prayerfully on God's presence during your day.

Gratitude

Grace

Review

Repent

Resolve

I'm grateful for

Prayer intentions

> "
> Contradictions bring us
> to the Foot of the Cross,
> and the Cross brings us
> to the Gates of Heaven.
>
> *St. John Vianney*

"

TO BE ALWAYS UNITED WITH JESUS, THIS IS MY PLAN OF LIFE.

B. Carlo Acutis

My prayer *journal*

Opening Prayer

Scripture & Reflection

Write down the Bible passage and your reflection.

Observation

Application

Apply God's Word to your life.

Today I will...

Prayer

Write down a prayer to God in response to His Word.

Pray the Examen

Reflect prayerfully on God's presence during your day.

Gratitude

Grace

Review

Repent

Resolve

My prayer journal

30 day challenge

Opening Prayer

Scripture & Reflection

Write down the Bible passage and your reflection.

Observation

Application

Apply God's Word to your life.

Today I will...

Prayer

Write down a prayer to God in response to His Word.

Pray the Examen

Reflect prayerfully on God's presence during your day.

Gratitude

Grace

Review

Repent

Resolve

My prayer *journal*

30 day challenge

🕊 Opening Prayer

Scripture & Reflection

Write down the Bible passage and your reflection.

Observation

Application

Apply God's Word to your life.

Today I will...

Prayer

Write down a prayer to God in response to His Word.

Pray the Examen

Reflect prayerfully on God's presence during your day.

Gratitude

Grace

Review

Repent

Resolve

My prayer journal

Opening Prayer

Scripture & Reflection
Write down the Bible passage and your reflection.

Observation

Application
Apply God's Word to your life.

Today I will...

Prayer

Write down a prayer to God in response to His Word.

Pray the Examen

Reflect prayerfully on God's presence during your day.

Gratitude

Grace

Review

Repent

Resolve

My prayer
journal

Opening Prayer

Date   S M T W T F S

30 day challenge

Scripture & Reflection

Write down the Bible passage and your reflection.

Observation

Application

Apply God's Word to your life.

Today I will...

Prayer

Write down a prayer to God in response to His Word.

Pray the Examen

Reflect prayerfully on God's presence during your day.

Gratitude

Grace

Review

Repent

Resolve

My prayer journal

Opening Prayer

30 day challenge

Scripture & Reflection
Write down the Bible passage and your reflection.

Observation

Application
Apply God's Word to your life.

Today I will...

Prayer

Write down a prayer to God in response to His Word.

Pray the Examen

Reflect prayerfully on God's presence during your day.

Gratitude

Grace

Review

Repent

Resolve

My prayer
journal

30 day challenge

Opening Prayer

Scripture & Reflection
Write down the Bible passage and your reflection.

Observation

Application
Apply God's Word to your life.

Today I will...

Prayer

Write down a prayer to God in response to His Word.

Pray the Examen

Reflect prayerfully on God's presence during your day.

Gratitude

Grace

Review

Repent

Resolve

OUR FATHER

I'm thankful for: *I ask you for:*

1
2
3
4
5
6
7
8
9
10

Especially: *Especially:*

"Prayer is the encounter of God's thirst with ours.
God thirsts that we may thirst for him."

St. Augustine

> Love is a mutual
> self-giving which ends
> in self-recovery.

V. Fulton J. Sheen

My prayer *journal*

30 day challenge

Opening Prayer

Scripture & Reflection
Write down the Bible passage and your reflection.

Observation

Application
Apply God's Word to your life.

Today I will...

Prayer

Write down a prayer to God in response to His Word.

Pray the Examen

Reflect prayerfully on God's presence during your day.

Gratitude

Grace

Review

Repent

Resolve

My prayer
journal

30 day challenge

Opening Prayer

Scripture & Reflection
Write down the Bible passage and your reflection.

Observation

Application
Apply God's Word to your life.

Today I will...

Prayer

Write down a prayer to God in response to His Word.

Pray the Examen

Reflect prayerfully on God's presence during your day.

Gratitude

Grace

Review

Repent

Resolve

My prayer
journal

30 day challenge

Opening Prayer

Scripture & Reflection

Write down the Bible passage and your reflection.

Observation

Application

Apply God's Word to your life.

Today I will...

Prayer

Write down a prayer to God in response to His Word.

Pray the Examen

Reflect prayerfully on God's presence during your day.

Gratitude

Grace

Review

Repent

Resolve

My prayer

journal

30 day challenge

Opening Prayer

Scripture & Reflection

Write down the Bible passage and your reflection.

Observation

Application

Apply God's Word to your life.

Today I will...

Prayer

Write down a prayer to God in response to His Word.

Pray the Examen

Reflect prayerfully on God's presence during your day.

Gratitude

Grace

Review

Repent

Resolve

My prayer
journal

30 day challenge

Opening Prayer

Scripture & Reflection
Write down the Bible passage and your reflection.

Observation

Application
Apply God's Word to your life.

Today I will...

Prayer

Write down a prayer to God in response to His Word.

Pray the Examen

Reflect prayerfully on God's presence during your day.

Gratitude

Grace

Review

Repent

Resolve

My prayer
journal

Opening Prayer

Scripture & Reflection
Write down the Bible passage and your reflection.

Observation

Application
Apply God's Word to your life.

Today I will...

Prayer

Write down a prayer to God in response to His Word.

Pray the Examen

Reflect prayerfully on God's presence during your day.

Gratitude

Grace

Review

Repent

Resolve

My prayer *journal*

30 day challenge

Opening Prayer

Scripture & Reflection

Write down the Bible passage and your reflection.

Observation

Application

Apply God's Word to your life.

Today I will...

Prayer

Write down a prayer to God in response to His Word.

Pray the Examen

Reflect prayerfully on God's presence during your day.

Gratitude

Grace

Review

Repent

Resolve

I'm grateful for

Prayer intentions

> **"**
> Prayer is the best gift
> you can give
> to those you love.
>
> *Mother Teresa*

"OUR HEART IS RESTLESS UNTIL IT RESTS IN YOU"

St. Augustine

My prayer
journal

Opening Prayer

Scripture & Reflection

Write down the Bible passage and your reflection.

Observation

Application

Apply God's Word to your life.

Today I will...

Prayer

Write down a prayer to God in response to His Word.

Pray the Examen

Reflect prayerfully on God's presence during your day.

Gratitude

Grace

Review

Repent

Resolve

My prayer journal

30 day challenge

Opening Prayer

Scripture & Reflection
Write down the Bible passage and your reflection.

Observation

Application
Apply God's Word to your life.

Today I will...

Prayer

Write down a prayer to God in response to His Word.

Pray the Examen

Reflect prayerfully on God's presence during your day.

Gratitude

Grace

Review

Repent

Resolve

My prayer
journal

30 day challenge

🕊 Opening Prayer

Scripture & Reflection
Write down the Bible passage and your reflection.

Observation

Application
Apply God's Word to your life.

Today I will...

Prayer

Write down a prayer to God in response to His Word.

Pray the Examen

Reflect prayerfully on God's presence during your day.

Gratitude

Grace

Review

Repent

Resolve

My prayer journal

30 day challenge

Opening Prayer

Scripture & Reflection
Write down the Bible passage and your reflection.

Observation

Application
Apply God's Word to your life.

Today I will...

Prayer

Write down a prayer to God in response to His Word.

Pray the Examen

Reflect prayerfully on God's presence during your day.

Gratitude

Grace

Review

Repent

Resolve

My prayer
journal

30 day challenge

Opening Prayer

Scripture & Reflection
Write down the Bible passage and your reflection.

Observation

Application
Apply God's Word to your life.

Today I will...

Prayer

Write down a prayer to God in response to His Word.

Pray the Examen

Reflect prayerfully on God's presence during your day.

Gratitude

Grace

Review

Repent

Resolve

My prayer
journal

30 day challenge

Opening Prayer

Scripture & Reflection
Write down the Bible passage and your reflection.

Observation

Application
Apply God's Word to your life.

Today I will...

Prayer

Write down a prayer to God in response to His Word.

Pray the Examen

Reflect prayerfully on God's presence during your day.

Gratitude

Grace

Review

Repent

Resolve

My prayer
journal

Date ⟨ S M T W T F S

30 day challenge

□□□□□□□□□□□□□□□□□□□□□□□□□□□□□□

Opening Prayer

Scripture & Reflection
Write down the Bible passage and your reflection.

Observation

Application
Apply God's Word to your life.

Today I will...

Prayer

Write down a prayer to God in response to His Word.

Pray the Examen

Reflect prayerfully on God's presence during your day.

Gratitude

Grace

Review

Repent

Resolve

OUR FATHER

I'm thankful for: *I ask you for:*

1

2

3

4

5

6

7

8

9

10

Especially: *Especially:*

"Prayer is in fact the recognition of our limits
and our dependence: we come from God,
we are of God, and to God we return."

St. John Paul II

> Spread love everywhere you go.
> Let no one ever come to you
> without leaving happier.
>
> *Mother Teresa of Calcutta*

My prayer
journal

30 day challenge

Opening Prayer

Scripture & Reflection
Write down the Bible passage and your reflection.

Observation

Application
Apply God's Word to your life.

Today I will...

Prayer

Write down a prayer to God in response to His Word.

Pray the Examen

Reflect prayerfully on God's presence during your day.

Gratitude

Grace

Review

Repent

Resolve

My prayer journal

30 day challenge

Opening Prayer

Scripture & Reflection
Write down the Bible passage and your reflection.

Observation

Application
Apply God's Word to your life.

Today I will...

Prayer

Write down a prayer to God in response to His Word.

Pray the Examen

Reflect prayerfully on God's presence during your day.

Gratitude

Grace

Review

Repent

Resolve

My prayer
journal

30 day challenge

Opening Prayer

Scripture & Reflection
Write down the Bible passage and your reflection.

Observation

Application
Apply God's Word to your life.

Today I will...

Prayer

Write down a prayer to God in response to His Word.

Pray the Examen

Reflect prayerfully on God's presence during your day.

Gratitude

Grace

Review

Repent

Resolve

My prayer
journal

30 day challenge

Opening Prayer

Scripture & Reflection
Write down the Bible passage and your reflection.

Observation

Application
Apply God's Word to your life.

Today I will...

Prayer

Write down a prayer to God in response to His Word.

Pray the Examen

Reflect prayerfully on God's presence during your day.

Gratitude

Grace

Review

Repent

Resolve

My prayer journal

30 day challenge

Opening Prayer

Scripture & Reflection

Write down the Bible passage and your reflection.

Observation

Application

Apply God's Word to your life.

Today I will...

Prayer

Write down a prayer to God in response to His Word.

Pray the Examen

Reflect prayerfully on God's presence during your day.

Gratitude

Grace

Review

Repent

Resolve

My prayer
journal

30 day challenge

Opening Prayer

Scripture & Reflection
Write down the Bible passage and your reflection.

Observation

Application
Apply God's Word to your life.

Today I will...

Prayer

Write down a prayer to God in response to His Word.

Pray the Examen

Reflect prayerfully on God's presence during your day.

Gratitude

Grace

Review

Repent

Resolve

My prayer
journal

30 day challenge

🕊 Opening Prayer

Scripture & Reflection
Write down the Bible passage and your reflection.

Observation

Application
Apply God's Word to your life.

Today I will...

Prayer

Write down a prayer to God in response to His Word.

Pray the Examen

Reflect prayerfully on God's presence during your day.

Gratitude

Grace

Review

Repent

Resolve

I'm grateful for

Prayer intentions

> 99
> Love is the inclination, strength, and power for the soul in making its way to God, for love unites it with God.
>
> *St. John of the Cross*

"NOTHING CAN HAPPEN TO ME THAT GOD DOESN'T WANT. AND ALL THAT HE WANTS, NO MATTER HOW BAD IT MAY APPEAR TO US, IS REALLY FOR THE BEST."

St. Thomas More

My prayer
journal

30 day challenge

Opening Prayer

Scripture & Reflection
Write down the Bible passage and your reflection.

Observation

Application
Apply God's Word to your life.

Today I will...

Prayer

Write down a prayer to God in response to His Word.

Pray the Examen

Reflect prayerfully on God's presence during your day.

Gratitude

Grace

Review

Repent

Resolve

My prayer
journal

30 day challenge

Opening Prayer

Scripture & Reflection
Write down the Bible passage and your reflection.

Observation

Application
Apply God's Word to your life.

Today I will...

Prayer

Write down a prayer to God in response to His Word.

Pray the Examen

Reflect prayerfully on God's presence during your day.

Gratitude

Grace

Review

Repent

Resolve

My prayer
journal

30 day challenge

Opening Prayer

Scripture & Reflection
Write down the Bible passage and your reflection.

Observation

Application
Apply God's Word to your life.

Today I will...

Prayer

Write down a prayer to God in response to His Word.

Pray the Examen

Reflect prayerfully on God's presence during your day.

Gratitude

Grace

Review

Repent

Resolve

My prayer *journal*

Date S M T W T F S

30 day challenge

Opening Prayer

Scripture & Reflection

Write down the Bible passage and your reflection.

Observation

Application

Apply God's Word to your life.

Today I will...

Prayer

Write down a prayer to God in response to His Word.

Pray the Examen

Reflect prayerfully on God's presence during your day.

Gratitude

Grace

Review

Repent

Resolve

My prayer
journal

30 day challenge

🕊 Opening Prayer

Scripture & Reflection
Write down the Bible passage and your reflection.

Observation

Application
Apply God's Word to your life.

Today I will...

Prayer

Write down a prayer to God in response to His Word.

Pray the Examen

Reflect prayerfully on God's presence during your day.

Gratitude

Grace

Review

Repent

Resolve

My prayer
journal

30 day challenge

Opening Prayer

Scripture & Reflection
Write down the Bible passage and your reflection.

Observation

Application
Apply God's Word to your life.

Today I will...

Prayer

Write down a prayer to God in response to His Word.

Pray the Examen

Reflect prayerfully on God's presence during your day.

Gratitude

Grace

Review

Repent

Resolve

My prayer journal

30 day challenge

Opening Prayer

Scripture & Reflection

Write down the Bible passage and your reflection.

Observation

Application

Apply God's Word to your life.

Today I will...

Prayer

Write down a prayer to God in response to His Word.

Pray the Examen

Reflect prayerfully on God's presence during your day.

Gratitude

Grace

Review

Repent

Resolve

OUR FATHER

1
2
3
4
5
6
7
8
9
10

Especially:

Especially:

"Have no anxiety at all, but in everything,
by prayer and petition, with thanksgiving,
make your requests known to God."

Philippians 4:6

"

The secret of happiness is to live
moment by moment and to thank
God for all that He, in His goodness,
sends to us day after day.

St. Gianna Beretta Molla

My prayer
journal

Opening Prayer

Scripture & Reflection
Write down the Bible passage and your reflection.

Observation

Application
Apply God's Word to your life.

Today I will...

Prayer

Write down a prayer to God in response to His Word.

Pray the Examen

Reflect prayerfully on God's presence during your day.

Gratitude

Grace

Review

Repent

Resolve

My prayer
journal

30 day challenge

🕊 Opening Prayer

Scripture & Reflection
Write down the Bible passage and your reflection.

Observation

Application
Apply God's Word to your life.

Today I will...

Prayer

Write down a prayer to God in response to His Word.

Pray the Examen

Reflect prayerfully on God's presence during your day.

Gratitude

Grace

Review

Repent

Resolve

My prayer
journal

30 day challenge

Opening Prayer

Scripture & Reflection
Write down the Bible passage and your reflection.

Observation

Application
Apply God's Word to your life.

Today I will...

Prayer

Write down a prayer to God in response to His Word.

Pray the Examen

Reflect prayerfully on God's presence during your day.

Gratitude

Grace

Review

Repent

Resolve

My prayer
journal

30 day challenge

Opening Prayer

Scripture & Reflection
Write down the Bible passage and your reflection.

Observation

Application
Apply God's Word to your life.

Today I will...

Prayer

Write down a prayer to God in response to His Word.

Pray the Examen

Reflect prayerfully on God's presence during your day.

Gratitude

Grace

Review

Repent

Resolve

My prayer
journal

30 day challenge

Opening Prayer

Scripture & Reflection

Write down the Bible passage and your reflection.

Observation

Application

Apply God's Word to your life.

Today I will...

Prayer

Write down a prayer to God in response to His Word.

Pray the Examen

Reflect prayerfully on God's presence during your day.

Gratitude

Grace

Review

Repent

Resolve

My prayer journal

30 day challenge

Opening Prayer

Scripture & Reflection

Write down the Bible passage and your reflection.

Observation

Application

Apply God's Word to your life.

Today I will...

Prayer

Write down a prayer to God in response to His Word.

Pray the Examen

Reflect prayerfully on God's presence during your day.

Gratitude

Grace

Review

Repent

Resolve

My prayer
journal

Opening Prayer

Date S M T W T F S

30 day challenge

Scripture & Reflection

Write down the Bible passage and your reflection.

Observation

Application

Apply God's Word to your life.

Today I will...

Prayer

Write down a prayer to God in response to His Word.

Pray the Examen

Reflect prayerfully on God's presence during your day.

Gratitude

Grace

Review

Repent

Resolve

I'm grateful for

Prayer intentions

- [ ]
- [ ]
- [ ]
- [ ]
- [ ]
- [ ]
- [ ]
- [ ]
- [ ]
- [ ]

> What food
> is to the body,
> prayer is to the soul.
>
> *St. Vincent de Paul*

"THE DEEDS YOU DO MAY BE THE ONLY SERMON SOME PERSONS WILL HEAR TODAY"

St. Francis of Assisi

My prayer
journal

30 day challenge

Opening Prayer

Scripture & Reflection
Write down the Bible passage and your reflection.

Observation

Application
Apply God's Word to your life.

Today I will...

Prayer

Write down a prayer to God in response to His Word.

Pray the Examen

Reflect prayerfully on God's presence during your day.

Gratitude

Grace

Review

Repent

Resolve

My prayer
journal

30 day challenge

Opening Prayer

Scripture & Reflection
Write down the Bible passage and your reflection.

Observation

Application
Apply God's Word to your life.

Today I will...

Prayer

Write down a prayer to God in response to His Word.

Pray the Examen

Reflect prayerfully on God's presence during your day.

Gratitude

Grace

Review

Repent

Resolve

My prayer journal

30 day challenge

Opening Prayer

Scripture & Reflection

Write down the Bible passage and your reflection.

Observation

Application

Apply God's Word to your life.

Today I will...

Prayer

Write down a prayer to God in response to His Word.

Pray the Examen

Reflect prayerfully on God's presence during your day.

Gratitude

Grace

Review

Repent

Resolve

My prayer
journal

Date S M T W T F S

30 day challenge

Opening Prayer

Scripture & Reflection

Write down the Bible passage and your reflection.

Observation

Application

Apply God's Word to your life.

Today I will...

Prayer

Write down a prayer to God in response to His Word.

Pray the Examen

Reflect prayerfully on God's presence during your day.

Gratitude

Grace

Review

Repent

Resolve

My prayer
journal

Date　S M T W T F S

30 day challenge

Opening Prayer

Scripture & Reflection
Write down the Bible passage and your reflection.

Observation

Application
Apply God's Word to your life.

Today I will...

Prayer

Write down a prayer to God in response to His Word.

Pray the Examen

Reflect prayerfully on God's presence during your day.

Gratitude

Grace

Review

Repent

Resolve

My prayer
journal

Opening Prayer

Date S M T W T F S

30 day challenge

Scripture & Reflection

Write down the Bible passage and your reflection.

Observation

Application

Apply God's Word to your life.

Today I will...

Prayer

Write down a prayer to God in response to His Word.

Pray the Examen

Reflect prayerfully on God's presence during your day.

Gratitude

Grace

Review

Repent

Resolve

My prayer
journal

30 day challenge

Opening Prayer

Scripture & Reflection

Write down the Bible passage and your reflection.

Observation

Application

Apply God's Word to your life.

Today I will...

Prayer

Write down a prayer to God in response to His Word.

Pray the Examen

Reflect prayerfully on God's presence during your day.

Gratitude

Grace

Review

Repent

Resolve

OUR FATHER

I'm thankful for: *I ask you for:*

1
2
3
4
5
6
7
8
9
10

Especially: *Especially:*

"Ponder the fact that God has made you a gardener,
to root out vice and plant virtue"

St Catherine of Siena

Whatever you do,
think of the Glory of God
as your main goal.

St. John Bosco

My prayer
journal

30 day challenge

Opening Prayer

Scripture & Reflection
Write down the Bible passage and your reflection.

Observation

Application
Apply God's Word to your life.

Today I will...

Prayer

Write down a prayer to God in response to His Word.

Pray the Examen

Reflect prayerfully on God's presence during your day.

Gratitude

Grace

Review

Repent

Resolve

My prayer
journal

30 day challenge

Opening Prayer

Scripture & Reflection
Write down the Bible passage and your reflection.

Observation

Application
Apply God's Word to your life.

Today I will...

Prayer

Write down a prayer to God in response to His Word.

Pray the Examen

Reflect prayerfully on God's presence during your day.

Gratitude

Grace

Review

Repent

Resolve

My prayer *journal*

30 day challenge

Opening Prayer

Scripture & Reflection

Write down the Bible passage and your reflection.

Observation

Application

Apply God's Word to your life.

Today I will...

Prayer

Write down a prayer to God in response to His Word.

Pray the Examen

Reflect prayerfully on God's presence during your day.

Gratitude

Grace

Review

Repent

Resolve

My prayer
journal

30 day challenge

Opening Prayer

Scripture & Reflection
Write down the Bible passage and your reflection.

Observation

Application
Apply God's Word to your life.

Today I will...

Prayer

Write down a prayer to God in response to His Word.

Pray the Examen

Reflect prayerfully on God's presence during your day.

Gratitude

Grace

Review

Repent

Resolve

My prayer journal

30 day challenge

▯▯▯▯▯▯▯▯▯▯▯▯▯▯▯▯▯▯▯▯▯▯▯▯▯▯▯▯▯▯

 Opening Prayer

Scripture & Reflection
Write down the Bible passage and your reflection.

Observation

Application
Apply God's Word to your life.

Today I will...

Prayer

Write down a prayer to God in response to His Word.

Pray the Examen

Reflect prayerfully on God's presence during your day.

Gratitude

Grace

Review

Repent

Resolve

My prayer journal

30 day challenge

Opening Prayer

Scripture & Reflection

Write down the Bible passage and your reflection.

Observation

Application

Apply God's Word to your life.

Today I will...

Prayer

Write down a prayer to God in response to His Word.

Pray the Examen

Reflect prayerfully on God's presence during your day.

Gratitude

Grace

Review

Repent

Resolve

My prayer
journal

30 day challenge

Opening Prayer

Scripture & Reflection
Write down the Bible passage and your reflection.

Observation

Application
Apply God's Word to your life.

Today I will...

Prayer

Write down a prayer to God in response to His Word.

Pray the Examen

Reflect prayerfully on God's presence during your day.

Gratitude

Grace

Review

Repent

Resolve

I'm grateful for

Prayer intentions

> "
> Every single grace
> comes to the soul
> through prayer.
>
> St. Faustina

"

NOT AS I, BUT AS YOU;
NOT WHEN I;
BUT WHEN YOU;
IF THAT IS YOUR WILL
THEN MY WILL IT IS
AS WELL

B. Conchita Cabrera de Armida

My prayer
journal

Date   S M T W T F S

30 day challenge

Opening Prayer

Scripture & Reflection
Write down the Bible passage and your reflection.

Observation

Application
Apply God's Word to your life.

Today I will...

Prayer

Write down a prayer to God in response to His Word.

Pray the Examen

Reflect prayerfully on God's presence during your day.

Gratitude

Grace

Review

Repent

Resolve

My prayer
journal

30 day challenge

Opening Prayer

Scripture & Reflection

Write down the Bible passage and your reflection.

Observation

Application

Apply God's Word to your life.

Today I will...

Prayer

Write down a prayer to God in response to His Word.

Pray the Examen

Reflect prayerfully on God's presence during your day.

Gratitude

Grace

Review

Repent

Resolve

My prayer
journal

30 day challenge

Opening Prayer

Scripture & Reflection

Write down the Bible passage and your reflection.

Observation

Application

Apply God's Word to your life.

Today I will...

Prayer

Write down a prayer to God in response to His Word.

Pray the Examen

Reflect prayerfully on God's presence during your day.

Gratitude

Grace

Review

Repent

Resolve

My prayer
journal

30 day challenge

Opening Prayer

Scripture & Reflection
Write down the Bible passage and your reflection.

Observation

Application
Apply God's Word to your life.

Today I will...

Prayer

Write down a prayer to God in response to His Word.

Pray the Examen

Reflect prayerfully on God's presence during your day.

Gratitude

Grace

Review

Repent

Resolve

My prayer journal

30 day challenge

Opening Prayer

Scripture & Reflection

Write down the Bible passage and your reflection.

Observation

Application

Apply God's Word to your life.

Today I will...

Prayer

Write down a prayer to God in response to His Word.

Pray the Examen

Reflect prayerfully on God's presence during your day.

Gratitude

Grace

Review

Repent

Resolve

My prayer journal

30 day challenge

Opening Prayer

Scripture & Reflection

Write down the Bible passage and your reflection.

Observation

Application

Apply God's Word to your life.

Today I will...

Prayer

Write down a prayer to God in response to His Word.

Pray the Examen

Reflect prayerfully on God's presence during your day.

Gratitude

Grace

Review

Repent

Resolve

My prayer
journal

Date S M T W T F S

30 day challenge

Opening Prayer

Scripture & Reflection
Write down the Bible passage and your reflection.

Observation

Application
Apply God's Word to your life.

Today I will...

Prayer

Write down a prayer to God in response to His Word.

_____

_____

_____

_____

_____

_____

_____

Pray the Examen

Reflect prayerfully on God's presence during your day.

Gratitude

Grace

Review

Repent

Resolve

OUR FATHER

I'm thankful for:

I ask you for:

1

2

3

4

5

6

7

8

9

10

Especially:

Especially:

"Don't ever forget to love."

St. Maximilian Kolbe

LET NOTHING DISTURB YOU,
LET NOTHING FRIGHTEN
YOU, ALL THINGS ARE
PASSING AWAY:
GOD NEVER CHANGES.
PATIENCE OBTAINS ALL
THINGS, WHOEVER
HAS GOD LACKS NOTHING;
GOD ALONE SUFFICES.

99

St. Teresa of Avila

NOVENA TRACKER

NOVENA:

INTENTIONS:

NOVENA:

INTENTIONS:

NOVENA:

INTENTIONS:

NOVENA:

INTENTIONS:

NOVENA TRACKER

NOVENA:

INTENTIONS:

_____
_____
_____

NOVENA:

INTENTIONS:

_____
_____
_____
_____

NOVENA:

INTENTIONS:

_____
_____
_____
_____

NOVENA:

INTENTIONS:

_____
_____
_____

NOVENA TRACKER

NOVENA:

INTENTIONS:

NOVENA:

INTENTIONS:

NOVENA:

INTENTIONS:

NOVENA:

INTENTIONS:

NOVENA TRACKER

NOVENA:

INTENTIONS:

NOVENA:

INTENTIONS:

NOVENA:

INTENTIONS:

NOVENA:

INTENTIONS:

Mysteries of the
ROSARY

Leader: In the Name of the Father, and of the Son, and of the Holy Spirit.
Participants: Amen

Leader: Lord Jesus Christ,
Participants: true God and man, my Creator and Redeemer, I love you above all else, and I am sorry with all my heart for offending you. To make up for my sins, which I firmly intend to confess in due time, I offer my life, my work, and all I do. I hope in your kindness and boundless mercy, and trust that you will forgive me and give me the grace never to offend you again. Amen

Leader: (The leader reads the general intention for the Rosary.)

Leader: Today we will reflect on the joyful mysteries.

Leader: The first mystery: The incarnation of the Son of God.

Reader: "'I am the Lord's servant,' said Mary, 'let what you have said be done to me'" (Luke 1:38).

Leader: The second mystery: Our Lady visits her cousin Elizabeth.

Reader: "Mary went into Zechariah's house and greeted Elizabeth" (Luke 1:40).

Leader: The third mystery: The birth of our Lord Jesus Christ.

Reader: "Mary gave birth to a son, her firstborn. She wrapped him in swaddling clothes and laid him in a manger" (Luke 2:7).

Leader: The fourth mystery: The presentation of the Lord in the Temple.

Reader: "Mary and Joseph took Jesus up to Jerusalem to present him to the Lord" (Luke 2:22).

Leader: The fifth mystery: The finding of Jesus in the Temple.

Reader: "Three days later, they found him in the Temple, sitting among the teachers" (Luke 2:46).

Leader: Hail Holy Queen and the Litany of Praise to the Blessed Virgin Mary.

Thursday

The Luminous Mysteries

Leader: Today we will reflect on the luminous mysteries.

Leader: The first mystery: The baptism of Jesus in the Jordan.

Reader: "And a voice spoke from heaven, 'This is my Son, the Beloved; my favor rests on him'" (Matthew 3:17).

Leader: The second mystery: Jesus reveals himself to his disciples at the wedding in Cana.

Reader: "This was the first of the signs given by Jesus: it was given at Cana in Galilee. He let his glory be seen, and his disciples believed in him" (John 2:11).

Leader: The third mystery: The proclamation of the Kingdom of God.

Reader: "Jesus went to Galilee. There he proclaimed the Good News from God. 'The time has come,' he said, 'and the Kingdom of God is close at hand. Repent, and believe the Good News'" (Mark 1:1415).

Leader: The fourth mystery: The transfiguration of Christ.

Reader: "As he prayed, he was transfigured in their presence: his face shone like the sun and his clothes became as white as the light" (Luke9:29;Matthew17:2).

Leader: The fifth mystery: The institution of the Eucharist.

Reader: "I am the living bread which has come down from heaven. Anyone who eats this bread will live for ever" (Jn 6:51).

Leader: Hail Holy Queen and the Litany of Praise to the Blessed Virgin Mary

Leader: Today we will reflect on the sorrowful mysteries.

Leader: The first mystery: The agony in the garden.

Reader: "In his anguish he prayed even more earnestly" (Luke 22:44).

Leader: The second mystery: The scourging at the pillar.

Reader: "Pilate then had Jesus taken away and scourged" (John 19:1).

Leader: The third mystery: The crowning with thorns.

Reader: "The soldiers twisted some thorns into a crown and put it on his head" (John 19:2).

Leader: The fourth mystery: Jesus carries his cross.

Reader: "Carrying his own cross, Jesus went out of the city to the place of the skull" (John 19:17).

Leader: The fifth mystery: Jesus dies on the cross.

Reader: "They crucified him with two others, one on either side with Jesus in the middle" (John 19:18).

Leader: Hail Holy Queen and the Litany of Praise to the Blessed Virgin Mary

The Glorious Mysteries

Wednesday and Sunday

Leader: Today we will reflect on the glorious mysteries.

Leader: The first mystery: The resurrection of the Lord.

Reader: "Why look among the dead for someone who is alive? He is not here, he has risen" (Luke 24:56).

Leader: The second mystery: The ascension of the Lord.

Reader: "As he blessed them, he withdrew from them and was carried up to heaven" (Luke 24:51).

Leader: The third mystery: The coming of the Holy Spirit on the apostles.

Reader: "Something appeared to them that seemed like tongues of fire; these separated and came to rest on the head of each of them. They were all filled with the Holy Spirit" (Acts 2:34).

Leader: The fourth mystery: The assumption of Mary into heaven.

Reader: "Blessed is she who believed that the promise made her by the Lord would be fulfilled" (Luke 1:45).

Leader: The fifth mystery: The coronation of Mary, Mother of the Church.

Reader: "A great sign appeared in heaven: a woman, adorned with the sun, standing on the moon, with twelve stars on her head for a crown" (Revelation 12:1).

Leader: Hail Holy Queen and the Litany of Praise to the Blessed Virgin Mary.

Litany of Praise
to the Blessed Virgin Mary

Lord, have mercy
Christ, have mercy
Lord, have mercy

God our Father in heaven
Have mercy on us.

God the Son, Redeemer of the world,
God the Holy Spirit
Holy Trinity, one God

Holy Mary
Pray for us.
Holy Mother of God
Most honored of virgins
Mother of Christ
Mother of the Church
Mother of divine grace
Mother most pure
Mother of chaste love
Mother and virgin
Sinless Mother
Dearest of mothers
Model of motherhood
Mother of good counsel
Mother of our Creator
Mother of our Savior
Mother of Regnum Christi
Virgin most wise
Virgin rightly praised
Virgin rightly renowned
Virgin most powerful
Virgin gentle in mercy
Faithful Virgin
Mirror of justice
Throne of wisdom
Cause of our joy
Shrine of the Spirit
Glory of Israel
Vessel of selfless devotion
Mystical Rose
Tower of David
Tower of ivory
House of gold
Ark of the covenant
Gate of heaven
Morning Star
Health of the sick,
Refuge of sinners

Comfort of the troubled
Help of Christians
Queen of angels
Queen of patriarchs and prophets
Queen of apostles and martyrs
Queen of confessors and virgins
Queen of all saints
Queen conceived without sin
Queen assumed into heaven
Queen of the Rosary
Queen of the family
Queen of peace

Lamb of God, you take away the sins of the world
Have mercy on us.

Lamb of God, you take away the sins of the world
Have mercy on us.

Lamb of God, you take away the sins of the world
Have mercy on us.

Pray for us, O holy Mother of God,
That we may be made worthy of the promises of Christ.

Let us pray:

O God, whose only begotten Son, by his life, death and resurrection, has purchased for us the rewards of eternal life, grant, we beseech thee, that meditating on these mysteries of the most holy Rosary of the Blessed Virgin Mary, we may imitate what they contain and obtain what they promise, through the same Christ our Lord.
Amen.

Made in the USA
Columbia, SC
20 April 2025

56894411R00124